Economics in Action

What is Importing and Exporting?

Gare Thompson

Crabtree Publishing Company

www.crabtreebooks.com

Crabtree Publishing Company

www.crabtreebooks.com

Author: Gare Thompson
Publishing plan research and development:
  Sean Charlebois, Reagan Miller
  Crabtree Publishing Company
Coordinating editor: Chester Fisher
Series editor: Gare Thompson Associates
Editor: Molly Aloian
Proofreader: Crystal Sikkens
Editorial director: Kathy Middleton
Production coordinator: Margaret Salter
Prepress technician: Margaret Salter
Project manager: Kumar Kunal (Q2AMEDIA)
Art direction: Harleen Mehta (Q2AMEDIA)
Cover design: Shruti Aggarwal (Q2AMEDIA)
Design: Shruti Aggarwal (Q2AMEDIA)
Photo research: Ekta Sharma (Q2AMEDIA)

Photographs:
123RF: George Spade: p. 8
AP Photo: Karel Prinsloo: p. 15 (bottom); Damian Dovarganes:
    title page, p. 23; Kin Cheung; p. 28; Eduardo Verdugo: p. 29
Corbis: Song Shi Jing/ Redlink: p. 19
Dreamstime: Aschwin Prein: p. 18 (bottom)
Istockphoto: Cherokeed: p. 21 (top)
Masterfile: p. 4, 5, 24
Photolibrary: KFS: p. 6; Bill Lai: p. 12; Moodboard: p. 16;
    Chris Cheadle: p. 22
Q2AMedia Art Bank: p. 17, 26
Reuters: Mick Tsikas: p. 13 (top); Stringer Iran: p. 17; Rebecca Cook:
    p. 20; Ho New: p. 21 (bottom)
Shutterstock: p.7 (left), 15 (middle), 18 (middle); Joy Brown: title
    page (left); Grzyn: p. 7 (right); Gator Dawg: p. 7 (bottom); Alsamua:
    p. 9 (top); Fedor Selivanov: p. 9 (middle); Andrejs Pidjass: p. 10;
    Christian Lagerek: p. 11; Andrew Donehue: p. 13 (bottom);
    J. Helgason: p. 18 (top); Dole: p. 25 (bottom left); Valery Potapova:
    p. 25 (bottom right); Artem Efimov: p. 27 (middle); Elnur: p. 27
    (bottom); Stephen Coburn: cover; Feng Yu: cover

Library and Archives Canada Cataloguing in Publication
Thompson, Gare
    What is importing and exporting? / Gare Thompson.

(Economics in action)
Includes index.
ISBN 978-0-7787-4443-6 (bound).--ISBN 978-0-7787-4454-2 (pbk.)

    1. International trade--Juvenile literature.
2. Imports--Juvenile literature. 3. Exports--Juvenile
literature. I. Title. II. Series: Economics in action
(St. Catherines, Ont.)

HF1379.T46 2010   j382   C2009-906267-4

Library of Congress Cataloging-in-Publication Data

Thompson, Gare.
What is importing and exporting? / Gare Thompson.
    p. cm. -- (Economics in action)
Includes index.
ISBN 978-0-7787-4454-2 (pbk. : alk. paper) -- ISBN 978-0-7787-4443-6
(reinforced library binding : alk. paper)
1. International trade--Juvenile literature. 2. Imports--Juvenile literature.
3. Exports--Juvenile literature. I. Title. II. Series.

HF1379.T487 2010
382--dc22

2009042774

Crabtree Publishing Company

www.crabtreebooks.com   1-800-387-7650
Printed in the USA/122009/BG20091103

Published in Canada
Crabtree Publishing
616 Welland Ave.
St. Catharines, ON
L2M 5V6

Published in the United States
Crabtree Publishing
PMB 59051
350 Fifth Avenue, 59th Floor
New York, New York 10118

Published in the United Kingdom
Crabtree Publishing
Maritime House
Basin Road North, Hove
BN41 1WR

Published in Australia
Crabtree Publishing
386 Mt. Alexander Rd.
Ascot Vale (Melbourne)
VIC 3032

Contents

Making a Trade

Your family car was manufactured in Japan. The shoes you love to wear were made in Italy. The bananas you put on your cereal are from Ecuador. Similarly, kids in Japan wear American jeans. People in Greece use wheat from Canada to make their bread. How did everyone get these different goods from other countries?

Countries around the world **trade** with one another. People or countries trade when they exchange **goods** and **services**. Goods are products, such as clothes, cars, or food. Services are actions or activities one person performs for another. For example, your doctor provides a service when you get your annual checkup.

▼ Countries trade for goods they need, such as cars.

Fair Trade

How do countries trade? Countries trade by **importing** and **exporting**. A country imports when it buys goods or services that it needs from other countries. A country exports when it sells goods or services to other countries that need them. Countries import and export goods around the world. This is called **international trade**. Here is how it works.

Ecuador has a good climate for growing bananas. The farmers in Ecuador can grow more bananas than its people can eat. The United States does not have the right climate or soil to grow bananas, but people in the United States want bananas.

▲ Ecuador is one of the largest exporters of bananas in the world. The United States is one of the largest importers of bananas.

So Ecuador exports bananas to the United States, and the United States imports bananas from Ecuador.

Although the farmers in Ecuador can grow plenty of bananas, they can't grow enough wheat to meet its people's needs. The people in Ecuador need wheat to make bread and other foods. The United States can grow a large supply of wheat, so the United States exports wheat to Ecuador. Ecuador and the United States trade bananas and wheat.

Point of Information

The United States imports and exports more goods than any other country in the world. In 2006, the United States imported almost $1.9 trillion goods. That same year, it exported over $1 trillion goods.

Imports, Exports, and You

Why do imports and exports matter to you? You are a **consumer**, or buyer. There are goods and services that you want, such as electronics and entertainment. There are also goods and services that you need, such as food and healthcare. If the things you want and need aren't made in your own country, then they must be imported from somewhere else. So, in a way, you help determine what your country imports.

Imports and You

Let's look at a specific example. Some people think Japan makes the best manga books, movies, and cartoons in the world. You are a big fan of these products. In fact, teens in countries around the world are huge consumers of Japanese manga. So teens have created a **demand** for manga merchandise. To meet this demand, different countries must import manga products from Japan, which has the **supply**.

▶ Manga products are popular imports with teens around the world.

Exports and You

It's pretty easy to see how your wants and needs affect what's imported. But what does the "export" side of the equation have to do with you? Here's one example. Your country exports electronics that are sold around the world. Factories have to produce a huge amount of product and therefore need a large number of workers. So because your country exports electronic products, you are able to get a summer job at one of those factories. Each time you cash your paycheck, be grateful for the countries that buy electronics from your country.

As you've seen, imports and exports are important to you, the consumer. The things you want to buy, the price you're willing to pay, and the quality you are willing to accept are all factors that help determine what your country imports. Similarly, what we export to other countries sometimes provides work and other benefits for you, your family, and your friends.

▲ Electronics are a product that many countries export.

Economics in Action

Some people think that imports hurt the country by eliminating jobs. In fact, the slogan "Made in the U.S.A." became a powerful way to help sell goods to U.S. citizens. Do you think consumers should only buy things made in their own countries?

What's Wrong with Home Grown?

So why doesn't every country simply grow or make what it needs and buy goods and services from its own citizens? Think about it. Can you make or provide everything you need to live? You need others to provide certain things for you. You can't grow all of your own food, make your own clothes, and produce everything you want. No one is that **self-sufficient**.

Countries work the same way. No single country can produce all the goods and services its citizens need. Countries may be lacking in one or more of the following areas:

Natural Resources

Natural resources are things that occur in nature that we can use. The water you drink and the gas you put in your car are examples of natural resources. Trees and minerals are examples of natural resources, too. Some of these resources are **scarce**, or limited, while others are plentiful. The natural resources a country has affects which goods and services it can produce and which it must import.

▶ This oil rig is drilling for oil. Oil is a limited resource.

8

A country's size, climate, and soil are the physical features that dictate which resources it has, which goods and services it can provide, and which ones it must import.

Think about an island country, such as Aruba. It has a warm climate with nice sandy beaches. Its resources make it a great place to vacation. The ocean waters surrounding Aruba are also perfect for fishing. So, fishing and tourism are **industries** that provide jobs and goods for its citizens. Aruba exports fish to other countries, and many people vacation in Aruba. However, the island does not have much farmland or mineral deposits so it has to import wheat and minerals.

▲ Water is a natural resource. It is scarce in a desert but plentiful in a rain forest.

Human Resources

Another factor that affects what countries import and export is **human resources**, or people. People provide the **labor**, or work, that is necessary to produce goods. The strength of a country's human resources is determined by the country's **population**, the education people receive, and the skills of the country's workers. All these factors affect what goods and services are produced.

Think about India. It is one of the most populous countries in the world, with a large number of well-educated people. In fact, Indian workers have a reputation for being particularly skilled in math, the sciences, and technology. This makes the workforce in India attractive to businesses around the world.

▼ Skilled labor is an important human resource.

Capital Resources

Capital resources are the buildings, machines, and tools needed to produce goods. Think of a car. To produce a car, many parts need to be **manufactured**. Factories filled with tools and equipment help make the parts so that cars can be produced.

Not all countries have the same kind or amount of capital resources. A country low in capital resources is dependent on other countries to supply it with tools and equipment or with the products made with those capital resources. China and the United States are examples of countries that are rich in capital resources. Many countries in Africa are low on capital resources and must depend on outside sources to get what they need.

Think about your own community. What kinds of resources are there? Do you have natural resources, such as forests or oceans, that make your area attractive to people from other areas? Do you have capital resources—factories or other industries that manufacture goods? Finally, do you have enough people to do the work that has to be done? All these factors help determine what goods and services your community produces, and what it needs to bring in.

▲ Machinery and tools are important capital resources.

▼ New Delhi, in India, has a population of over 17 million people.

Point of Information

India's population is well over 1 billion people. India is the second most populous country in the world.

11

The Rich Get Richer...

You are part of a local community in the same way that countries around the world are part of a global community. You depend on your community to meet your wants and needs. You are affected by how rich or poor your community is.

Countries, too, are linked through their wants and needs. Each country's **economy** affects not only its own citizens, but those of other countries. This **interdependency** means that the more resources a country has, the more power or control it can have over countries that don't have those resources.

Countries who are strong in all three kinds of resources—natural, human, and capital—are in the best position when it comes to exporting products and making a **profit**. Australia is a good example. It has many different natural resources, but one of the most important is coal. The country has vast supplies of coal. It also has the capital and human resources to mine and process it.

▼ Australia is also the fourth largest exporter of wine. This vineyard is in New South Wales, Australia.

Developed Countries

However, other countries around the world don't have much or any coal, but need it for power plants, turbines, and other equipment. So coal has become one of Australia's top exports. Not only that, but Australia is able to set a high price for its coal because other countries need it so much. The profit helps pay for many of the goods Australia imports, and also allows it to continue to build and develop its own capital resources. A rich country gets richer.

Countries such as Australia, that are rich in all three resources—natural, human, and capital—are called **developed countries**. Developed countries often have economic and political power over other countries that need their goods.

▲ Australia is the third largest exporter of coal in the world. Every state in Australia has a coal mine.

▼ Opals are a luxury item.

Point of Information

Australia exports other minerals. For example, it is the number one exporter of opals in the world.

▲ Less-developed countries have fewer resources.

Less-Developed Countries

But what about countries that aren't rich? Think of it this way. Imagine you live in a desert. Your supply of water is very limited so you can grow only a few crops. You don't have the money to buy irrigation equipment that would allow you to raise more crops. You're not trained to do other work. Your resources are limited, and you can't produce goods to sell. You need help from outside your country.

Some countries are in a similar situation. They are called **less-developed countries**. Less-developed countries often have fewer natural resources, untrained labor, and few capital resources. They may also be held back by internal conflicts, such as civil wars or corrupt leadership. In any case, they have little to export and limited ways to make money. Without money they can't buy goods or services from richer countries. They are likely to have few industries and a low standard of living. Unlike richer countries, they do not have the resources to make products, export goods, and make profits. They can't grow, and they can't improve their standard of living. The poor get poorer.

An example of a less-developed country is the Republic of Chad. Chad is a landlocked country in Africa. It has few natural resources, since most of the country is a desert. Few of its people are trained for jobs or have much education. It does not have a secure government, so civil wars often break out. Its lack of resources gives Chad little to export. However, oil has been discovered in Chad. If the means can be found to drill for and export this oil, the country may finally have the resources to help itself grow.

▼ Farmers in Chad have few capital resources.

The Big Players

Countries import and export goods based on their supply of resources. Over time, some countries have grown powerful because they have a great supply of resources. Countries that export products that other countries need, such as oil, coal, or crops, gain power over the countries that need those goods to survive. The exporting countries and regions are the "big players" in the world market.

The United States

The United States is a big player because of its rich resources. It has natural resources, such as minerals and crops, that other countries need. Its people are well-educated and trained. U.S. workers produce many different goods and offer services that other countries want. The U.S. has the capital resources to buy equipment needed to produce goods, such as electronics. It also has cities, parks, and museums that attract tourists, which create many jobs. The United States works to help less-developed countries by sending them food and medical supplies. When countries depend on the United States for goods and services, the U.S. acquires economic and political power over those countries.

▲ The United States uses its many ports to ship its exports to countries around the world.

▲ Saudi Arabia exports the most oil of any country in the Middle East.

The Middle East

Think of oil and you think of the Middle East. The Middle East contains more than half of the world's **oil reserves**. Since other nations need oil for fuel, heating, and manufacturing, oil has been the major export of this region since 1908, when the supplies were first discovered. The profits from oil provide the Middle East with money to improve the lives of its people and keep its economy strong. Oil also gives the Middle East a great deal of political power. Other countries can't risk offending the leaders of those countries and losing access to the oil supply. However, the Middle East has little soil good for farming and few factories that produce goods. As a result, it imports food and most manufactured goods. The Middle East's profits from its oil exports help pay for its imports.

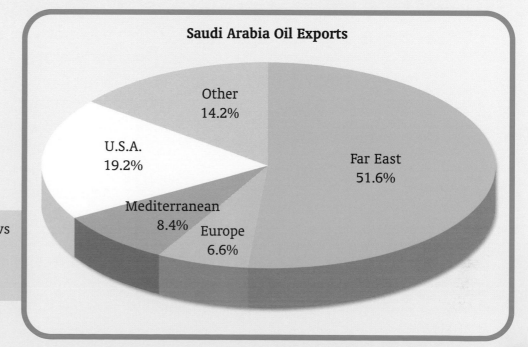

Saudi Arabia Oil Exports

Other 14.2%

U.S.A. 19.2%

Far East 51.6%

Mediterranean 8.4%

Europe 6.6%

▶ This circle graph shows Saudi Arabia exports the most oil to countries in the Far East.

Africa

Many countries in Africa are rich in minerals and other resources. North Africa has rich oil reserves, so that region exports petroleum which is used to make oil and gas. Ghana was once called the Gold Coast because it exported so much gold. However, one mineral has made Africa famous. It is the diamond. South Africa is one of the top producers of diamonds in the world. Other minerals that African countries export are coal, copper, and iron. Many countries around the world need these minerals for their factories. Iron is used to make steel, while diamonds are used in everything from jewelry to tools. Its natural resources make many African nations big players.

▼ Many countries in Africa export minerals.

▼ The Three Gorges Dam in China is the largest dam that generates electricity in the world.

Asia

Asia has rich resources, which have made many of the countries there major players in the world economy. For example, China and India have large populations that provide a powerful work force. Their workers manufacture goods and offer services other countries need, and often produce them at a lower price. Asia also has a tremendous amount of capital resources, which enable countries such as India, Japan, and China to produce electronics, cars, toys, and clothes that are exported around the world.

Asia also has a wealth of natural resources. One of its most important is water. A number of Asian nations have built dams along its rivers to produce **hydroelectricity**, which helps power its industries. Many countries also border oceans, so fishing has become an important industry and a profitable export. A third resource, oil, is also showing great potential. Every day, in China's Takla Makan Desert region, workers battle the desert heat and sand as they drill and collect oil. Scientists believe that the region has huge reserves. China hopes to become a major producer and exporter of oil, which will increase Asia's importance in the world economy.

Point of Information

The Takla Makan Desert region is also called the "Sea of Death." The only people who live in the area work for oil companies.

▼ The huge oil reserves in the Takla Makan Desert will make China a major supplier of oil.

When Power Shifts

Over time, the economic power of countries can shift. Some countries may lose power, while others may gain power.

Some of the things that may cause a shift are
- dwindling natural resources;
- advances in technology;
- changing needs and wants of consumers;
- a natural disaster, such as a hurricane or flood;
- a war or other conflict.

Let's look at two countries and see how their economic power has changed over time.

▼ Advances in technology help countries produce more goods faster and cheaper.

The United Arab Emirates (Dubai)

Dubai is a desert country. It does not have farmland. In the early 1900s, the few people who lived there were nomads. They moved constantly across the desert, herding goats. The country was very poor. In 1966, oil was discovered in Dubai. Suddenly, the country had a powerful resource to export. Other countries needed Dubai's oil. Once Dubai began exporting oil, it became rich. It had money to build schools, roads, and modern communication systems. Today, Dubai is a big tourist attraction with beautiful hotels and restaurants. However, Dubai does have to import many goods and services, including skilled workers. Oil is a **nonrenewable resource**. Dubai will run out of oil in time. When it does, its power may decline.

▲ Dubai is a modern city.

The Philippines

From the 1950s until the 1990s, the Philippines was one of the leading exporters of wood. It had vast forests, which it logged. Since many countries needed wood for building and other uses, the Philippines was a strong country with important economic power.

Trees are a **renewable resource**. New trees can be planted. However, it takes years for trees to grow and replace the forests that were cut down. From 1990 to 1999, over 75,000 acres (30,351 hectares) of trees were cut down in the Philippines. Few new trees were planted. As a result, the Philippines ran out of this natural resource. Instead of exporting wood, it now imports wood, which has created a dramatic shift in its economy. There is less money coming in, and many jobs have been lost.

▼ Once forests have been cut down, it takes many years for the trees to grow back.

21

Maintaining a Balance

Let's say you earn $100 a month. You try to spend less than that each month so that you can save for emergencies or a special purchase. In other words, you work to balance your earning and spending. Countries must balance what they earn and what they spend, too.

Countries can achieve a balance through their imports and exports. Ideally, countries want to sell more than they buy. This balance keeps the country's internal economy strong. People in the country are working, earning money, and purchasing goods and services. Balance also helps a country maintain the value of its money outside its borders. That money can be used to purchase goods and services from other countries at a good rate. Let's look at some things that affect a country's balance of imports and exports.

Surplus and Deficit

You have probably heard about surplus and deficit, but what do the terms mean? Countries try to export more than they import. In other words, they want to sell more goods than they buy. When this happens the country has a **trade surplus**.

Canada often has a trade surplus. It exports more goods, including beef and gas, than it imports.

◀ Beef is one of Canada's top exports.

◀ Oil accounts for almost 40 percent of all energy used in the U.S. today.

Canada is also able to sell its products at good prices, while buying products at reasonable prices. So it makes a solid profit.

What if a country imports more than it exports? Well, if you spend more than you earn, you are in **debt**—you owe money. It works the same way for a country. If a country imports more than it exports, then it runs a **trade deficit**. This means the country is buying more goods than it is selling.

The United States has had a trade deficit since the late 1960s. It currently imports more goods than it exports. One of its main imports is oil. The United States is dependent on other countries, such as Canada and Saudi Arabia, for oil.

But is a trade deficit always bad? Does it mean a country is broke? No, trade deficits are not always bad. Trade works when both parties are happy with their exchange. Often, imported goods cost more than goods produced locally. This may increase the demand for local goods because they are cheaper. Increased demand means more jobs for local people. They earn money and spend it. This keeps the economy strong and provides the money the country needs to pay for imports.

Point of Information

In 2007, the United States imported more goods from its top five trading partners (Canada, Mexico, Germany, Japan, and China) than it exported to them.

Foreign Exchange Rate

How are imports and exports connected to a country's money? The value of a country's **currency** is determined in part by how much the country imports and exports. The value of a country's money compared to other countries is called the **foreign exchange rate**.

The foreign exchange rate helps determine how much a country pays for goods it buys from other countries. A country's position in the global economy is affected by the exchange rate of its money. A strong currency means that a country can get more for its money. A weak currency means it gets much less.

Let's say the United States wants to buy oil from Mexico. The price of Mexican oil is calculated in Mexican pesos. So if the U.S. dollar is stronger than the Mexican peso, the United States can buy more oil with its dollars. But if the Mexican peso is stronger than the U.S. dollar, then the United States will buy less oil for the same amount of dollars. Countries buy goods where they can get the most for their money. So it pays to know what the foreign exchange rate is!

▲ When your country's currency is strong, you can buy more goods that are imported from other countries.

Exchange Rates as of October 20, 2009	
Currency	Amount equal to 1 U.S. dollar
Canadian Dollar	1.050062
Chinese Yuan	6.828000
Euro	0.670955
Japanese Yen	90.83550
Mexican Peso	12.96348

Source: http://moneycentral.msn.com

Gross Domestic Product (GDP)

So how do countries know if their economy is doing well or not? One way is to look at the **gross domestic product** (GDP). The GDP is the value of all the goods and services made within the country at their current prices. It accounts for every sneaker, television, car, and all other goods made that year. It tracks a country's exports. Why is it important?

Countries look at their GDP to find out how well they are doing economically. Their GDP tells them which of their products are most profitable. It helps determine how strong the country's currency is and if an increase or decrease in employment is likely.

The GDP also allows countries to compare themselves with other countries. It tells them what countries they should buy products from and what they may need to invest in. It also tells them who to sell to and how much they can sell. The GDP and its data helps governments to make important economic decisions.

Point of Information

All countries track their GDP. In the United States, the Department of Commerce tracks this data. For example, it tracks employment during a particular period to find out how many workers lost their jobs and how many new jobs were created. This helps the government decide what industries it needs to support in order to create new jobs.

▼ Governments track the products their countries produce.

The Government Steps In

Companies in the United States make cars. Japan makes and exports cars to the United States. How can the United States make sure its own car manufacturers can compete in the car market?

Think of a police officer directing the flow of traffic. He or she makes sure that the lines of cars take turns, and that no street becomes too backed up.

Governments also use warnings and laws to maintain their economy. Just as the officer controlled the flow of traffic, governments control the flow of goods between countries. They do this to protect local farmers, manufacturers, and consumers.

Governments control the flow of goods in a number of ways. These methods are referred to as **trade barriers** because they sometimes stop or slow the flow of trade.

Import Quotas

Let's return to the idea of the production of cars. To protect car makers in the United States, the U.S. has put an **import quota** on automobiles. An import quota limits the quantity of a good that can be imported, in this case, cars. This helps the local car manufacturers and dealers because the market will not be flooded with cars from other countries.

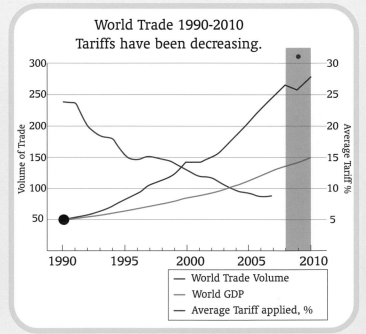

World Trade 1990-2010
Tariffs have been decreasing.

— World Trade Volume
— World GDP
— Average Tariff applied, %

Tariffs

Tariffs are taxes put on goods when they are transported across a political boundary (usually from one country to another). Tariffs raise the price of the good being imported and make it easier for local producers to compete. Since local producers don't have to pay a tariff, they can charge less for their products.

Licenses

Licenses are papers showing legal permission to sell certain products, such as alcohol, tobacco, firearms, and other items that are under the control of government agencies. Countries that export those products need licenses with the government agency that monitors them.

Export Taxes

Some countries place an **export tax** on goods that are shipped out of the country. This tax causes the price of the product to go down within the country but go up in the rest of the world. For example, Russia uses export taxes on petroleum. This keeps the price of petroleum lower within Russia but higher in the rest of the world. The United States Constitution prevents the U.S. government from using this trade barrier.

Trade Embargoes

Trade embargoes are a way to stop imports and exports to a country. They are usually used to punish a country for real or imagined bad behavior. In 2007, the United States had trade embargoes against Cuba, Iran, and Myanmar (Burma). Most embargoes are imposed because of human rights violations or terrorism.

▼ Countries often put tariffs on baby clothes and shoes. Do you think tariffs can help or hurt a country?

Globalization

Today, countries are part of a world community. Countries depend on each other more now than they did in the past. They need to work together.

Countries exchange ideas, culture, and goods every day. This exchange is called **globalization**. How do countries keep trade fair? They turn to the World Trade Organization (WTO). It works to help countries trade fairly and openly.

So how does the WTO work? Leaders of countries gather at trade **summits**, or meetings, to resolve trade issues. They discuss lowering tariffs, ending import quotas, and protecting less-developed countries. They try to resolve labor issues that affect global imports and exports. The WTO settles trade disputes and works out trade agreements between countries.

▼ World leaders gather in China at the WTO Conference to make trade agreements.

For example, in 2005 Mexico complained to the WTO that Panama had imposed a new tariff on milk products that was unfair. The two countries met with WTO. Working with WTO, the two countries agreed on a tariff that was fair to both countries.

Trade Agreements

Canada, the United States, and Mexico are neighbors. In 1994, the three countries signed a trade agreement. They now trade together under an agreement called the North American Free Trade Agreement (NAFTA). NAFTA's main purpose is to remove most trade barriers and increase investment opportunities in the three countries. Similarly, the European Union (the countries in Europe that work together) has several free trade agreements with countries around the world, including Mexico.

Imports and exports are an important part of every country's economy. They are also important to you, the consumer. Exports often provide jobs, goods, and services. Imports provide goods you couldn't find in your country. You, the consumer, affect what goods are imported and exported. As the world becomes more global, countries work together to make sure imports and exports work for all.

▲ Mexican farmers protest against the removal of import tariffs on corn from the U.S. and Canada.

Point of Information

Not all people like the trade agreements such as NAFTA. In February 2008, thousands of Mexican farmers gathered in Mexico City with a herd of cattle and more than 50 tractors to protest the NAFTA decision to remove the tarrif on corn from the United States and Canada. The farmers stated that they would not be able to compete with the cheap corn from the U.S. and Canada. The Mexican government promised to look at ways to help the farmers.

Glossary

capital resources The buildings, machines, and tools needed to produce goods

consumer A person who buys and uses things

currency The money used in a country

debt Something that is owed to another

demand What people want to buy

developed country A country that has built its resources into industries to make products that are exported to other countries and uses its profits to expand and build on its resources

economy The way a country produces, distributes, and uses its money, goods, natural resources, and services

export To send goods to other countries to be sold or traded

export tax An extra payment to the government on goods that are shipped out of the country; used as a trade barrier

foreign exchange rate The value of a country's money compared to other countries

globalization Countries around the world exchanging ideas, culture, and goods

goods Any object a person wants or needs to help them survive

gross domestic product (GDP) The total value of goods and services produced within a country

human resources The knowledge and skills that workers have

hydroelectricity Power created by generators run by rapidly flowing water

import To bring in goods from another country for sale or use

import quota Rules that limit the quantity of a good that can be imported in order to protect local farmers or merchants who grow or produce the same good

industry A branch of business, trade, or manufacturing

international trade Countries importing and exporting goods around the world

interdependency Each country's economy affects that of other countries; the more resources a country has, the more power it is likely to have over countries with fewer resources

labor The work that goes into making a good or performing a service